50 Best Mac and Cheese Recipes

By: Kelly Johnson

Table of Contents

- Classic Mac and Cheese
- Truffle Mac and Cheese
- Lobster Mac and Cheese
- Bacon Mac and Cheese
- Buffalo Chicken Mac and Cheese
- BBQ Pulled Pork Mac and Cheese
- Spicy Jalapeño Mac and Cheese
- Mac and Cheese with Crispy Panko
- Creamy Gouda and Cheddar Mac and Cheese
- Baked Mac and Cheese with Bread Crumbs
- Mac and Cheese with Sausage and Peppers
- Veggie Mac and Cheese
- Mac and Cheese with Roasted Garlic
- Smoked Gouda Mac and Cheese
- Spinach and Artichoke Mac and Cheese
- White Cheddar Mac and Cheese
- Cajun Chicken Mac and Cheese

- Mac and Cheese with Caramelized Onions
- Mac and Cheese with Truffle Oil
- Mac and Cheese with Ground Beef
- Pesto Mac and Cheese
- Mac and Cheese with Roasted Tomatoes
- Mac and Cheese with BBQ Chicken
- Mac and Cheese with Broccoli
- Crab Mac and Cheese
- Mac and Cheese with Caramelized Bacon
- Pepper Jack Mac and Cheese
- Mac and Cheese with Fried Chicken
- Mac and Cheese with Sauteed Mushrooms
- Mac and Cheese with Brussel Sprouts
- Blue Cheese Mac and Cheese
- Mac and Cheese with Hot Dogs
- Mac and Cheese with Fried Onions
- Mac and Cheese with Sweet Potatoes
- Mac and Cheese with Shrimp
- Mac and Cheese with Chorizo

- Mac and Cheese with Ham
- Mac and Cheese with Kielbasa
- Sriracha Mac and Cheese
- Smoked Salmon Mac and Cheese
- Mac and Cheese with Parmesan and Truffle Butter
- Mac and Cheese with Spinach and Bacon
- Mac and Cheese with Roasted Cauliflower
- Mac and Cheese with Gouda and Bacon
- Vegan Mac and Cheese
- Mac and Cheese with Lobster and Crab
- Mac and Cheese with Duck Confit
- Mac and Cheese with Applewood Smoked Bacon
- Mac and Cheese with Kale and Sausage
- Mac and Cheese with Sweet Corn and Jalapeños

Classic Mac and Cheese

Ingredients:

- 8 oz elbow macaroni
- 2 cups shredded sharp cheddar cheese
- 1/2 cup grated Parmesan cheese
- 2 cups whole milk
- 2 tbsp butter
- 2 tbsp all-purpose flour
- 1 tsp mustard powder
- Salt and pepper to taste
- 1/2 tsp garlic powder (optional)
- 1/4 tsp paprika (optional)

Instructions:

1. Cook the macaroni according to package instructions, drain, and set aside.
2. In a saucepan, melt the butter over medium heat. Stir in the flour and cook for 1-2 minutes to create a roux.
3. Gradually whisk in the milk, ensuring no lumps form. Bring to a simmer, then cook for 3-5 minutes until the sauce thickens.
4. Stir in the cheddar and Parmesan cheeses, mustard powder, garlic powder, paprika, salt, and pepper. Stir until the cheese melts and the sauce is smooth.
5. Add the cooked macaroni to the cheese sauce and stir to combine. Serve warm.

Truffle Mac and Cheese

Ingredients:

- 8 oz elbow macaroni
- 2 cups shredded Gruyère cheese
- 1/2 cup shredded Parmesan cheese
- 2 cups heavy cream
- 2 tbsp butter
- 1 tbsp truffle oil
- 1 tbsp all-purpose flour
- Salt and pepper to taste
- 1/4 cup fresh breadcrumbs (for topping)

Instructions:

1. Cook the macaroni according to package instructions, drain, and set aside.
2. In a saucepan, melt the butter over medium heat. Stir in the flour and cook for 1-2 minutes to create a roux.
3. Gradually whisk in the heavy cream, and cook for 3-5 minutes until the sauce thickens.
4. Stir in the Gruyère, Parmesan, salt, and pepper. Add the truffle oil and stir until the sauce is smooth and the cheese has melted.
5. Toss the cooked macaroni in the cheese sauce.
6. For a crispy topping, place the mac and cheese in an oven-safe dish, sprinkle breadcrumbs on top, and bake at 350°F (175°C) for 10-15 minutes until golden

brown.

Lobster Mac and Cheese

Ingredients:

- 8 oz elbow macaroni
- 2 lobster tails (cooked and chopped)
- 2 cups shredded sharp cheddar cheese
- 1/2 cup grated Parmesan cheese
- 2 cups whole milk
- 2 tbsp butter
- 2 tbsp all-purpose flour
- Salt and pepper to taste
- 1/4 tsp paprika (optional)
- 1/4 tsp garlic powder (optional)
- 1/2 cup breadcrumbs (for topping)

Instructions:

1. Cook the macaroni according to package instructions, drain, and set aside.
2. In a saucepan, melt the butter over medium heat. Stir in the flour and cook for 1-2 minutes.
3. Gradually whisk in the milk, and cook for 3-5 minutes until the sauce thickens.
4. Stir in the cheddar, Parmesan, salt, pepper, paprika, and garlic powder. Once the cheese has melted, add the chopped lobster.

5. Toss the cooked macaroni in the cheese sauce and lobster mixture.

6. Top with breadcrumbs and bake at 350°F (175°C) for 10-15 minutes until the top is golden and crispy.

Bacon Mac and Cheese

Ingredients:

- 8 oz elbow macaroni
- 1/2 lb bacon (cooked and chopped)
- 2 cups shredded sharp cheddar cheese
- 1/2 cup grated Parmesan cheese
- 2 cups whole milk
- 2 tbsp butter
- 2 tbsp all-purpose flour
- Salt and pepper to taste
- 1/2 cup breadcrumbs (for topping)

Instructions:

1. Cook the macaroni according to package instructions, drain, and set aside.
2. Cook the bacon until crispy, then chop it into small pieces.
3. In a saucepan, melt the butter over medium heat. Stir in the flour and cook for 1-2 minutes.
4. Gradually whisk in the milk, and cook for 3-5 minutes until the sauce thickens.
5. Stir in the cheddar, Parmesan, salt, and pepper. Once the cheese has melted, add the cooked bacon.
6. Toss the cooked macaroni in the cheese sauce and bacon mixture.

7. Top with breadcrumbs and bake at 350°F (175°C) for 10-15 minutes until the top is golden and crispy.

Buffalo Chicken Mac and Cheese

Ingredients:

- 8 oz elbow macaroni
- 2 cups shredded cheddar cheese
- 1/2 cup blue cheese crumbles
- 2 cups whole milk
- 2 tbsp butter
- 2 tbsp all-purpose flour
- 1 cup cooked chicken (shredded)
- 1/4 cup buffalo sauce
- Salt and pepper to taste
- 1/2 cup breadcrumbs (for topping)

Instructions:

1. Cook the macaroni according to package instructions, drain, and set aside.
2. In a saucepan, melt the butter over medium heat. Stir in the flour and cook for 1-2 minutes.
3. Gradually whisk in the milk, and cook for 3-5 minutes until the sauce thickens.
4. Stir in the cheddar, blue cheese, salt, and pepper. Once the cheese has melted, add the shredded chicken and buffalo sauce.
5. Toss the cooked macaroni in the cheese sauce and chicken mixture.

6. Top with breadcrumbs and bake at 350°F (175°C) for 10-15 minutes until the top is golden and crispy.

BBQ Pulled Pork Mac and Cheese

Ingredients:

- 8 oz elbow macaroni
- 2 cups shredded sharp cheddar cheese
- 1/2 cup grated Parmesan cheese
- 2 cups whole milk
- 2 tbsp butter
- 2 tbsp all-purpose flour
- 1 cup pulled pork (cooked and shredded)
- 1/4 cup BBQ sauce
- Salt and pepper to taste
- 1/2 cup breadcrumbs (for topping)

Instructions:

1. Cook the macaroni according to package instructions, drain, and set aside.
2. In a saucepan, melt the butter over medium heat. Stir in the flour and cook for 1-2 minutes.
3. Gradually whisk in the milk, and cook for 3-5 minutes until the sauce thickens.
4. Stir in the cheddar, Parmesan, salt, and pepper. Once the cheese has melted, add the pulled pork and BBQ sauce.
5. Toss the cooked macaroni in the cheese sauce and pulled pork mixture.

6. Top with breadcrumbs and bake at 350°F (175°C) for 10-15 minutes until the top is golden and crispy.

Spicy Jalapeño Mac and Cheese

Ingredients:

- 8 oz elbow macaroni
- 2 cups shredded sharp cheddar cheese
- 1/2 cup cream cheese
- 2 cups whole milk
- 2 tbsp butter
- 2 tbsp all-purpose flour
- 1-2 fresh jalapeños (sliced)
- 1/4 tsp cayenne pepper (optional)
- Salt and pepper to taste
- 1/2 cup breadcrumbs (for topping)

Instructions:

1. Cook the macaroni according to package instructions, drain, and set aside.
2. In a saucepan, melt the butter over medium heat. Stir in the flour and cook for 1-2 minutes.
3. Gradually whisk in the milk, and cook for 3-5 minutes until the sauce thickens.
4. Stir in the cheddar, cream cheese, cayenne pepper, salt, and pepper. Once the cheese has melted, add the jalapeños.
5. Toss the cooked macaroni in the cheese sauce and jalapeño mixture.

6. Top with breadcrumbs and bake at 350°F (175°C) for 10-15 minutes until the top is golden and crispy.

Mac and Cheese with Crispy Panko

Ingredients:

- 8 oz elbow macaroni
- 2 cups shredded sharp cheddar cheese
- 1/2 cup grated Parmesan cheese
- 2 cups whole milk
- 2 tbsp butter
- 2 tbsp all-purpose flour
- Salt and pepper to taste
- 1 cup panko breadcrumbs (for topping)
- 1 tbsp olive oil (for crispy topping)

Instructions:

1. Cook the macaroni according to package instructions, drain, and set aside.
2. In a saucepan, melt the butter over medium heat. Stir in the flour and cook for 1-2 minutes.
3. Gradually whisk in the milk, and cook for 3-5 minutes until the sauce thickens.
4. Stir in the cheddar, Parmesan, salt, and pepper. Once the cheese has melted, toss the cooked macaroni in the cheese sauce.
5. In a small pan, heat olive oil over medium heat. Add the panko breadcrumbs and toast until golden and crispy.
6. Top the mac and cheese with the crispy panko breadcrumbs and serve warm.

Creamy Gouda and Cheddar Mac and Cheese

Ingredients:

- 8 oz elbow macaroni
- 1 cup shredded Gouda cheese
- 1 cup shredded sharp cheddar cheese
- 2 cups heavy cream
- 2 tbsp butter
- 2 tbsp all-purpose flour
- Salt and pepper to taste
- 1/4 tsp smoked paprika (optional)
- 1/2 cup breadcrumbs (for topping)

Instructions:

1. Cook the macaroni according to package instructions, drain, and set aside.
2. In a saucepan, melt the butter over medium heat. Stir in the flour and cook for 1-2 minutes.
3. Gradually whisk in the heavy cream, and cook for 3-5 minutes until the sauce thickens.
4. Stir in the Gouda, cheddar, smoked paprika, salt, and pepper. Once the cheese has melted, toss the cooked macaroni in the cheese sauce.
5. Top with breadcrumbs and bake at 350°F (175°C) for 10-15 minutes until the top is golden and crispy.

Baked Mac and Cheese with Bread Crumbs

Ingredients:

- 8 oz elbow macaroni
- 2 cups shredded sharp cheddar cheese
- 1/2 cup grated Parmesan cheese
- 2 cups whole milk
- 2 tbsp butter
- 2 tbsp all-purpose flour
- Salt and pepper to taste
- 1/2 cup breadcrumbs (for topping)
- 1 tbsp butter (for breadcrumb topping)

Instructions:

1. Cook the macaroni according to package instructions, drain, and set aside.
2. In a saucepan, melt the butter over medium heat. Stir in the flour and cook for 1-2 minutes.
3. Gradually whisk in the milk, and cook for 3-5 minutes until the sauce thickens.
4. Stir in the cheddar, Parmesan, salt, and pepper. Once the cheese has melted, toss the cooked macaroni in the cheese sauce.
5. Pour the mac and cheese mixture into a greased baking dish. Top with breadcrumbs and dot with the extra butter.
6. Bake at 350°F (175°C) for 15-20 minutes or until the top is golden and crispy.

Mac and Cheese with Sausage and Peppers

Ingredients:

- 8 oz elbow macaroni
- 2 cups shredded sharp cheddar cheese
- 1/2 cup grated Parmesan cheese
- 2 cups whole milk
- 2 tbsp butter
- 2 tbsp all-purpose flour
- 1 lb sausage (Italian or breakfast, cooked and crumbled)
- 1 bell pepper, diced
- 1/2 onion, diced
- Salt and pepper to taste
- 1/2 tsp crushed red pepper flakes (optional)

Instructions:

1. Cook the macaroni according to package instructions, drain, and set aside.
2. In a skillet, cook the sausage until browned, then remove and set aside.
3. In the same skillet, sauté the bell pepper and onion until softened.
4. In a saucepan, melt the butter over medium heat. Stir in the flour and cook for 1-2 minutes.
5. Gradually whisk in the milk, and cook for 3-5 minutes until the sauce thickens.

6. Stir in the cheddar, Parmesan, salt, pepper, and red pepper flakes. Once the cheese has melted, add the sausage and sautéed vegetables.

7. Toss the cooked macaroni in the cheese sauce and sausage mixture, and serve warm.

Veggie Mac and Cheese

Ingredients:

- 8 oz elbow macaroni
- 2 cups shredded sharp cheddar cheese
- 1/2 cup grated Parmesan cheese
- 2 cups whole milk
- 2 tbsp butter
- 2 tbsp all-purpose flour
- 1 cup broccoli florets (steamed or sautéed)
- 1/2 cup diced carrots (steamed or sautéed)
- 1/2 cup peas
- Salt and pepper to taste

Instructions:

1. Cook the macaroni according to package instructions, drain, and set aside.
2. In a saucepan, melt the butter over medium heat. Stir in the flour and cook for 1-2 minutes.
3. Gradually whisk in the milk, and cook for 3-5 minutes until the sauce thickens.
4. Stir in the cheddar, Parmesan, salt, and pepper. Once the cheese has melted, add the cooked veggies (broccoli, carrots, and peas).
5. Toss the cooked macaroni in the cheese sauce and veggie mixture, and serve warm.

Mac and Cheese with Roasted Garlic

Ingredients:

- 8 oz elbow macaroni
- 2 cups shredded sharp cheddar cheese
- 1/2 cup grated Parmesan cheese
- 2 cups whole milk
- 2 tbsp butter
- 2 tbsp all-purpose flour
- 4 cloves roasted garlic (mashed)
- Salt and pepper to taste
- 1/4 tsp garlic powder (optional)

Instructions:

1. Cook the macaroni according to package instructions, drain, and set aside.
2. In a saucepan, melt the butter over medium heat. Stir in the flour and cook for 1-2 minutes.
3. Gradually whisk in the milk, and cook for 3-5 minutes until the sauce thickens.
4. Stir in the cheddar, Parmesan, mashed roasted garlic, garlic powder, salt, and pepper. Once the cheese has melted, toss the cooked macaroni in the garlic cheese sauce, and serve warm.

Smoked Gouda Mac and Cheese

Ingredients:

- 8 oz elbow macaroni
- 1 cup shredded smoked Gouda cheese
- 1 cup shredded sharp cheddar cheese
- 2 cups whole milk
- 2 tbsp butter
- 2 tbsp all-purpose flour
- Salt and pepper to taste
- 1/4 tsp smoked paprika (optional)

Instructions:

1. Cook the macaroni according to package instructions, drain, and set aside.
2. In a saucepan, melt the butter over medium heat. Stir in the flour and cook for 1-2 minutes.
3. Gradually whisk in the milk, and cook for 3-5 minutes until the sauce thickens.
4. Stir in the Gouda, cheddar, smoked paprika, salt, and pepper. Once the cheese has melted, toss the cooked macaroni in the cheese sauce and serve warm.

Spinach and Artichoke Mac and Cheese

Ingredients:

- 8 oz elbow macaroni
- 2 cups shredded sharp cheddar cheese
- 1/2 cup grated Parmesan cheese
- 2 cups whole milk
- 2 tbsp butter
- 2 tbsp all-purpose flour
- 1 cup spinach (fresh or frozen, sautéed or steamed)
- 1 cup artichoke hearts (canned or jarred, chopped)
- Salt and pepper to taste

Instructions:

1. Cook the macaroni according to package instructions, drain, and set aside.
2. In a saucepan, melt the butter over medium heat. Stir in the flour and cook for 1-2 minutes.
3. Gradually whisk in the milk, and cook for 3-5 minutes until the sauce thickens.
4. Stir in the cheddar, Parmesan, salt, and pepper. Once the cheese has melted, add the spinach and artichokes.
5. Toss the cooked macaroni in the cheese sauce and veggie mixture, and serve warm.

White Cheddar Mac and Cheese

Ingredients:

- 8 oz elbow macaroni
- 2 cups shredded white cheddar cheese
- 1/2 cup grated Parmesan cheese
- 2 cups whole milk
- 2 tbsp butter
- 2 tbsp all-purpose flour
- Salt and pepper to taste
- 1/4 tsp garlic powder (optional)

Instructions:

1. Cook the macaroni according to package instructions, drain, and set aside.
2. In a saucepan, melt the butter over medium heat. Stir in the flour and cook for 1-2 minutes.
3. Gradually whisk in the milk, and cook for 3-5 minutes until the sauce thickens.
4. Stir in the white cheddar, Parmesan, salt, pepper, and garlic powder. Once the cheese has melted, toss the cooked macaroni in the cheese sauce and serve warm.

Cajun Chicken Mac and Cheese

Ingredients:

- 8 oz elbow macaroni
- 2 cups shredded sharp cheddar cheese
- 1/2 cup grated Parmesan cheese
- 2 cups whole milk
- 2 tbsp butter
- 2 tbsp all-purpose flour
- 1 lb chicken breast (cooked and diced)
- 1 tbsp Cajun seasoning
- Salt and pepper to taste

Instructions:

1. Cook the macaroni according to package instructions, drain, and set aside.
2. In a skillet, cook the chicken until browned and fully cooked. Toss with Cajun seasoning.
3. In a saucepan, melt the butter over medium heat. Stir in the flour and cook for 1-2 minutes.
4. Gradually whisk in the milk, and cook for 3-5 minutes until the sauce thickens.
5. Stir in the cheddar, Parmesan, salt, and pepper. Once the cheese has melted, add the cooked chicken.

6. Toss the cooked macaroni in the cheese sauce and Cajun chicken mixture, and serve warm.

Mac and Cheese with Caramelized Onions

Ingredients:

- 8 oz elbow macaroni
- 2 cups shredded sharp cheddar cheese
- 1/2 cup grated Parmesan cheese
- 2 cups whole milk
- 2 tbsp butter
- 2 tbsp all-purpose flour
- 2 medium onions (thinly sliced)
- 1 tbsp olive oil
- Salt and pepper to taste

Instructions:

1. Cook the macaroni according to package instructions, drain, and set aside.
2. In a skillet, heat olive oil over medium-low heat. Add the onions and cook for 20-30 minutes, stirring occasionally, until caramelized.
3. In a saucepan, melt the butter over medium heat. Stir in the flour and cook for 1-2 minutes.
4. Gradually whisk in the milk, and cook for 3-5 minutes until the sauce thickens.
5. Stir in the cheddar, Parmesan, salt, and pepper. Once the cheese has melted, add the caramelized onions.
6. Toss the cooked macaroni in the cheese sauce and caramelized onions, and serve warm.

Mac and Cheese with Truffle Oil

Ingredients:

- 8 oz elbow macaroni
- 2 cups shredded sharp cheddar cheese
- 1/2 cup grated Parmesan cheese
- 2 cups whole milk
- 2 tbsp butter
- 2 tbsp all-purpose flour
- 1 tbsp truffle oil
- Salt and pepper to taste
- 1/4 tsp garlic powder (optional)

Instructions:

1. Cook the macaroni according to package instructions, drain, and set aside.
2. In a saucepan, melt the butter over medium heat. Stir in the flour and cook for 1-2 minutes.
3. Gradually whisk in the milk, and cook for 3-5 minutes until the sauce thickens.
4. Stir in the cheddar, Parmesan, salt, pepper, and garlic powder. Once the cheese has melted, drizzle in the truffle oil and stir to combine.
5. Toss the cooked macaroni in the cheese sauce and serve warm.

Mac and Cheese with Ground Beef

Ingredients:

- 8 oz elbow macaroni
- 2 cups shredded sharp cheddar cheese
- 1/2 cup grated Parmesan cheese
- 2 cups whole milk
- 2 tbsp butter
- 2 tbsp all-purpose flour
- 1 lb ground beef (cooked and drained)
- Salt and pepper to taste

Instructions:

1. Cook the macaroni according to package instructions, drain, and set aside.
2. In a skillet, cook the ground beef until browned, then drain any excess fat.
3. In a saucepan, melt the butter over medium heat. Stir in the flour and cook for 1-2 minutes.
4. Gradually whisk in the milk, and cook for 3-5 minutes until the sauce thickens.
5. Stir in the cheddar, Parmesan, salt, and pepper. Once the cheese has melted, add the cooked ground beef.
6. Toss the cooked macaroni in the cheese sauce and ground beef mixture, and serve warm.

Pesto Mac and Cheese

Ingredients:

- 8 oz elbow macaroni
- 2 cups shredded mozzarella cheese
- 1/2 cup grated Parmesan cheese
- 2 cups whole milk
- 2 tbsp butter
- 2 tbsp all-purpose flour
- 1/4 cup basil pesto (store-bought or homemade)
- Salt and pepper to taste

Instructions:

1. Cook the macaroni according to package instructions, drain, and set aside.
2. In a saucepan, melt the butter over medium heat. Stir in the flour and cook for 1-2 minutes.
3. Gradually whisk in the milk, and cook for 3-5 minutes until the sauce thickens.
4. Stir in the mozzarella, Parmesan, pesto, salt, and pepper. Once the cheese has melted, toss the cooked macaroni in the cheese sauce and serve warm.

Mac and Cheese with Roasted Tomatoes

Ingredients:

- 8 oz elbow macaroni
- 2 cups shredded sharp cheddar cheese
- 1/2 cup grated Parmesan cheese
- 2 cups whole milk
- 2 tbsp butter
- 2 tbsp all-purpose flour
- 1 cup cherry tomatoes (halved)
- 1 tbsp olive oil
- Salt and pepper to taste

Instructions:

1. Preheat your oven to 400°F (200°C). Toss the halved cherry tomatoes with olive oil, salt, and pepper, and roast for 20-25 minutes until soft and caramelized.

2. Cook the macaroni according to package instructions, drain, and set aside.

3. In a saucepan, melt the butter over medium heat. Stir in the flour and cook for 1-2 minutes.

4. Gradually whisk in the milk, and cook for 3-5 minutes until the sauce thickens.

5. Stir in the cheddar, Parmesan, salt, and pepper. Once the cheese has melted, fold in the roasted tomatoes.

6. Toss the cooked macaroni in the cheese sauce and roasted tomatoes, and serve warm.

Mac and Cheese with BBQ Chicken

Ingredients:

- 8 oz elbow macaroni
- 2 cups shredded sharp cheddar cheese
- 1/2 cup grated Parmesan cheese
- 2 cups whole milk
- 2 tbsp butter
- 2 tbsp all-purpose flour
- 2 cups cooked chicken breast (shredded)
- 1/4 cup BBQ sauce
- Salt and pepper to taste

Instructions:

1. Cook the macaroni according to package instructions, drain, and set aside.
2. In a skillet, cook the shredded chicken with BBQ sauce until heated through and caramelized.
3. In a saucepan, melt the butter over medium heat. Stir in the flour and cook for 1-2 minutes.
4. Gradually whisk in the milk, and cook for 3-5 minutes until the sauce thickens.
5. Stir in the cheddar, Parmesan, salt, and pepper. Once the cheese has melted, fold in the BBQ chicken.

6. Toss the cooked macaroni in the cheese sauce and BBQ chicken mixture, and serve warm.

Mac and Cheese with Broccoli

Ingredients:

- 8 oz elbow macaroni
- 2 cups shredded sharp cheddar cheese
- 1/2 cup grated Parmesan cheese
- 2 cups whole milk
- 2 tbsp butter
- 2 tbsp all-purpose flour
- 1 cup broccoli florets (steamed or blanched)
- Salt and pepper to taste

Instructions:

1. Cook the macaroni according to package instructions, drain, and set aside.
2. In a saucepan, melt the butter over medium heat. Stir in the flour and cook for 1-2 minutes.
3. Gradually whisk in the milk, and cook for 3-5 minutes until the sauce thickens.
4. Stir in the cheddar, Parmesan, salt, and pepper. Once the cheese has melted, fold in the steamed broccoli.

5. Toss the cooked macaroni in the cheese sauce and broccoli mixture, and serve warm.

Crab Mac and Cheese

Ingredients:

- 8 oz elbow macaroni
- 2 cups shredded sharp cheddar cheese
- 1/2 cup grated Parmesan cheese
- 2 cups whole milk
- 2 tbsp butter
- 2 tbsp all-purpose flour
- 1/2 lb lump crab meat (fresh or canned)
- Salt and pepper to taste
- 1/4 tsp paprika (optional)

Instructions:

1. Cook the macaroni according to package instructions, drain, and set aside.
2. In a saucepan, melt the butter over medium heat. Stir in the flour and cook for 1-2 minutes.
3. Gradually whisk in the milk, and cook for 3-5 minutes until the sauce thickens.

4. Stir in the cheddar, Parmesan, salt, pepper, and paprika. Once the cheese has melted, fold in the crab meat.

5. Toss the cooked macaroni in the cheese sauce and crab mixture, and serve warm.

Mac and Cheese with Caramelized Bacon

Ingredients:

- 8 oz elbow macaroni
- 2 cups shredded sharp cheddar cheese
- 1/2 cup grated Parmesan cheese
- 2 cups whole milk
- 2 tbsp butter
- 2 tbsp all-purpose flour
- 4 strips bacon (cooked and crumbled)
- 1 tbsp brown sugar (for caramelizing bacon)
- Salt and pepper to taste

Instructions:

1. Cook the macaroni according to package instructions, drain, and set aside.
2. In a skillet, cook the bacon until crispy. Remove from the skillet, and crumble it.

3. In the same skillet, add brown sugar and cook the bacon crumbles until caramelized.

4. In a saucepan, melt the butter over medium heat. Stir in the flour and cook for 1-2 minutes.

5. Gradually whisk in the milk, and cook for 3-5 minutes until the sauce thickens.

6. Stir in the cheddar, Parmesan, salt, and pepper. Once the cheese has melted, fold in the caramelized bacon.

7. Toss the cooked macaroni in the cheese sauce and caramelized bacon, and serve warm.

Pepper Jack Mac and Cheese

Ingredients:

- 8 oz elbow macaroni
- 2 cups shredded pepper jack cheese
- 1/2 cup grated cheddar cheese
- 2 cups whole milk
- 2 tbsp butter
- 2 tbsp all-purpose flour
- Salt and pepper to taste
- 1/4 tsp cayenne pepper (optional for extra heat)

Instructions:

1. Cook the macaroni according to package instructions, drain, and set aside.

2. In a saucepan, melt the butter over medium heat. Stir in the flour and cook for 1-2 minutes.

3. Gradually whisk in the milk, and cook for 3-5 minutes until the sauce thickens.

4. Stir in the pepper jack cheese, cheddar, salt, pepper, and cayenne pepper. Once the cheese has melted, toss the cooked macaroni in the cheese sauce and serve warm.

Mac and Cheese with Fried Chicken

Ingredients:

- 8 oz elbow macaroni
- 2 cups shredded sharp cheddar cheese
- 1/2 cup grated Parmesan cheese
- 2 cups whole milk
- 2 tbsp butter
- 2 tbsp all-purpose flour
- 1 lb fried chicken (cut into bite-sized pieces)
- Salt and pepper to taste

Instructions:

1. Cook the macaroni according to package instructions, drain, and set aside.
2. In a saucepan, melt the butter over medium heat. Stir in the flour and cook for 1-2 minutes.
3. Gradually whisk in the milk, and cook for 3-5 minutes until the sauce thickens.
4. Stir in the cheddar, Parmesan, salt, and pepper. Once the cheese has melted, toss in the fried chicken pieces.
5. Toss the cooked macaroni in the cheese sauce and fried chicken, and serve warm.

Mac and Cheese with Sautéed Mushrooms

Ingredients:

- 8 oz elbow macaroni
- 2 cups shredded sharp cheddar cheese
- 1/2 cup grated Parmesan cheese
- 2 cups whole milk
- 2 tbsp butter
- 2 tbsp all-purpose flour
- 2 cups mushrooms (sliced and sautéed)
- Salt and pepper to taste

Instructions:

1. Cook the macaroni according to package instructions, drain, and set aside.
2. In a skillet, sauté the sliced mushrooms with a little butter until tender and golden brown. Set aside.
3. In a saucepan, melt the butter over medium heat. Stir in the flour and cook for 1-2 minutes.
4. Gradually whisk in the milk, and cook for 3-5 minutes until the sauce thickens.
5. Stir in the cheddar, Parmesan, salt, and pepper. Once the cheese has melted, fold in the sautéed mushrooms.
6. Toss the cooked macaroni in the cheese sauce and mushroom mixture, and serve warm.

Mac and Cheese with Brussel Sprouts

Ingredients:

- 8 oz elbow macaroni
- 2 cups shredded sharp cheddar cheese
- 1/2 cup grated Parmesan cheese
- 2 cups whole milk
- 2 tbsp butter
- 2 tbsp all-purpose flour
- 1 cup Brussels sprouts (trimmed, halved, and roasted)
- Salt and pepper to taste

Instructions:

1. Preheat the oven to 400°F (200°C). Toss the Brussels sprouts with olive oil, salt, and pepper, and roast for 20-25 minutes until crispy and caramelized.
2. Cook the macaroni according to package instructions, drain, and set aside.
3. In a saucepan, melt the butter over medium heat. Stir in the flour and cook for 1-2 minutes.
4. Gradually whisk in the milk, and cook for 3-5 minutes until the sauce thickens.
5. Stir in the cheddar, Parmesan, salt, and pepper. Once the cheese has melted, fold in the roasted Brussels sprouts.
6. Toss the cooked macaroni in the cheese sauce and Brussels sprouts, and serve warm.

Blue Cheese Mac and Cheese

Ingredients:

- 8 oz elbow macaroni
- 1 cup shredded sharp cheddar cheese
- 1 cup crumbled blue cheese
- 2 cups whole milk
- 2 tbsp butter
- 2 tbsp all-purpose flour
- Salt and pepper to taste

Instructions:

1. Cook the macaroni according to package instructions, drain, and set aside.
2. In a saucepan, melt the butter over medium heat. Stir in the flour and cook for 1-2 minutes.
3. Gradually whisk in the milk, and cook for 3-5 minutes until the sauce thickens.
4. Stir in the cheddar, blue cheese, salt, and pepper. Once the cheese has melted, toss the cooked macaroni in the cheese sauce and serve warm.

Mac and Cheese with Hot Dogs

Ingredients:

- 8 oz elbow macaroni
- 2 cups shredded sharp cheddar cheese
- 1/2 cup grated Parmesan cheese
- 2 cups whole milk
- 2 tbsp butter
- 2 tbsp all-purpose flour
- 4 hot dogs (sliced into rounds)
- Salt and pepper to taste

Instructions:

1. Cook the macaroni according to package instructions, drain, and set aside.
2. In a skillet, sauté the sliced hot dogs until lightly browned and heated through. Set aside.
3. In a saucepan, melt the butter over medium heat. Stir in the flour and cook for 1-2 minutes.
4. Gradually whisk in the milk, and cook for 3-5 minutes until the sauce thickens.
5. Stir in the cheddar, Parmesan, salt, and pepper. Once the cheese has melted, fold in the sautéed hot dogs.
6. Toss the cooked macaroni in the cheese sauce and hot dogs, and serve warm.

Mac and Cheese with Fried Onions

Ingredients:

- 8 oz elbow macaroni
- 2 cups shredded sharp cheddar cheese
- 1/2 cup grated Parmesan cheese
- 2 cups whole milk
- 2 tbsp butter
- 2 tbsp all-purpose flour
- 1 cup fried onions (store-bought or homemade)
- Salt and pepper to taste

Instructions:

1. Cook the macaroni according to package instructions, drain, and set aside.
2. In a saucepan, melt the butter over medium heat. Stir in the flour and cook for 1-2 minutes.
3. Gradually whisk in the milk, and cook for 3-5 minutes until the sauce thickens.
4. Stir in the cheddar, Parmesan, salt, and pepper. Once the cheese has melted, fold in the fried onions.
5. Toss the cooked macaroni in the cheese sauce and fried onions, and serve warm.

Mac and Cheese with Sweet Potatoes

Ingredients:

- 8 oz elbow macaroni
- 2 cups shredded sharp cheddar cheese
- 1/2 cup grated Parmesan cheese
- 2 cups whole milk
- 2 tbsp butter
- 2 tbsp all-purpose flour
- 1 cup roasted sweet potatoes (mashed)
- Salt and pepper to taste

Instructions:

1. Preheat the oven to 400°F (200°C). Roast sweet potatoes for 30-40 minutes until tender, then peel and mash.
2. Cook the macaroni according to package instructions, drain, and set aside.
3. In a saucepan, melt the butter over medium heat. Stir in the flour and cook for 1-2 minutes.
4. Gradually whisk in the milk, and cook for 3-5 minutes until the sauce thickens.
5. Stir in the cheddar, Parmesan, salt, pepper, and mashed sweet potatoes. Once the cheese has melted, toss the cooked macaroni in the cheese sauce and sweet potatoes, and serve warm.

Mac and Cheese with Shrimp

Ingredients:

- 8 oz elbow macaroni
- 2 cups shredded sharp cheddar cheese
- 1/2 cup grated Parmesan cheese
- 2 cups whole milk
- 2 tbsp butter
- 2 tbsp all-purpose flour
- 1 lb shrimp (peeled and deveined)
- Salt, pepper, and paprika to taste

Instructions:

1. Cook the macaroni according to package instructions, drain, and set aside.
2. In a skillet, sauté the shrimp with butter, salt, pepper, and paprika until cooked through. Set aside.
3. In a saucepan, melt the butter over medium heat. Stir in the flour and cook for 1-2 minutes.
4. Gradually whisk in the milk, and cook for 3-5 minutes until the sauce thickens.
5. Stir in the cheddar, Parmesan, salt, and pepper. Once the cheese has melted, fold in the cooked shrimp.
6. Toss the cooked macaroni in the cheese sauce and shrimp, and serve warm.

Mac and Cheese with Chorizo

Ingredients:

- 8 oz elbow macaroni
- 2 cups shredded sharp cheddar cheese
- 1/2 cup grated Parmesan cheese
- 2 cups whole milk
- 2 tbsp butter
- 2 tbsp all-purpose flour
- 1/2 lb chorizo (crumbled and cooked)
- Salt and pepper to taste

Instructions:

1. Cook the macaroni according to package instructions, drain, and set aside.
2. In a skillet, cook the crumbled chorizo until browned and crispy. Set aside.
3. In a saucepan, melt the butter over medium heat. Stir in the flour and cook for 1-2 minutes.
4. Gradually whisk in the milk, and cook for 3-5 minutes until the sauce thickens.
5. Stir in the cheddar, Parmesan, salt, and pepper. Once the cheese has melted, fold in the cooked chorizo.
6. Toss the cooked macaroni in the cheese sauce and chorizo, and serve warm.

Mac and Cheese with Ham

Ingredients:

- 8 oz elbow macaroni
- 2 cups shredded sharp cheddar cheese
- 1/2 cup grated Parmesan cheese
- 2 cups whole milk
- 2 tbsp butter
- 2 tbsp all-purpose flour
- 1 cup diced ham (cooked)
- Salt and pepper to taste

Instructions:

1. Cook the macaroni according to package instructions, drain, and set aside.
2. In a saucepan, melt the butter over medium heat. Stir in the flour and cook for 1-2 minutes.
3. Gradually whisk in the milk, and cook for 3-5 minutes until the sauce thickens.
4. Stir in the cheddar, Parmesan, salt, and pepper. Once the cheese has melted, fold in the diced ham.
5. Toss the cooked macaroni in the cheese sauce and ham mixture, and serve warm.

Mac and Cheese with Kielbasa

Ingredients:

- 8 oz elbow macaroni
- 2 cups shredded sharp cheddar cheese
- 1/2 cup grated Parmesan cheese
- 2 cups whole milk
- 2 tbsp butter
- 2 tbsp all-purpose flour
- 2 kielbasa sausages (sliced)
- Salt and pepper to taste

Instructions:

1. Cook the macaroni according to package instructions, drain, and set aside.
2. In a skillet, sauté the kielbasa slices until browned and crispy. Set aside.
3. In a saucepan, melt the butter over medium heat. Stir in the flour and cook for 1-2 minutes.
4. Gradually whisk in the milk, and cook for 3-5 minutes until the sauce thickens.
5. Stir in the cheddar, Parmesan, salt, and pepper. Once the cheese has melted, fold in the sautéed kielbasa.
6. Toss the cooked macaroni in the cheese sauce and kielbasa, and serve warm.

Sriracha Mac and Cheese

Ingredients:

- 8 oz elbow macaroni
- 2 cups shredded sharp cheddar cheese
- 1/2 cup grated Parmesan cheese
- 2 cups whole milk
- 2 tbsp butter
- 2 tbsp all-purpose flour
- 2 tbsp Sriracha sauce (adjust to taste)
- Salt and pepper to taste

Instructions:

1. Cook the macaroni according to package instructions, drain, and set aside.
2. In a saucepan, melt the butter over medium heat. Stir in the flour and cook for 1-2 minutes.
3. Gradually whisk in the milk, and cook for 3-5 minutes until the sauce thickens.
4. Stir in the cheddar, Parmesan, Sriracha sauce, salt, and pepper. Once the cheese has melted, toss the cooked macaroni in the cheese sauce and serve warm.

Smoked Salmon Mac and Cheese

Ingredients:

- 8 oz elbow macaroni
- 2 cups shredded sharp cheddar cheese
- 1/2 cup grated Parmesan cheese
- 2 cups whole milk
- 2 tbsp butter
- 2 tbsp all-purpose flour
- 1/2 lb smoked salmon (flaked)
- 1 tbsp capers (optional)
- Salt and pepper to taste

Instructions:

1. Cook the macaroni according to package instructions, drain, and set aside.
2. In a saucepan, melt the butter over medium heat. Stir in the flour and cook for 1-2 minutes.
3. Gradually whisk in the milk, and cook for 3-5 minutes until the sauce thickens.
4. Stir in the cheddar, Parmesan, salt, and pepper. Once the cheese has melted, fold in the smoked salmon and capers (if using).
5. Toss the cooked macaroni in the cheese sauce and salmon mixture, and serve warm.

Mac and Cheese with Parmesan and Truffle Butter

Ingredients:

- 8 oz elbow macaroni
- 2 cups shredded Parmesan cheese
- 1/2 cup grated Gruyère cheese (optional)
- 2 cups whole milk
- 2 tbsp butter
- 2 tbsp truffle butter
- 2 tbsp all-purpose flour
- Salt and pepper to taste

Instructions:

1. Cook the macaroni according to package instructions, drain, and set aside.
2. In a saucepan, melt the butter and truffle butter over medium heat. Stir in the flour and cook for 1-2 minutes.
3. Gradually whisk in the milk, and cook for 3-5 minutes until the sauce thickens.
4. Stir in the Parmesan, Gruyère (if using), salt, and pepper. Once the cheese has melted, toss the cooked macaroni in the cheese sauce and serve warm.

Mac and Cheese with Spinach and Bacon

Ingredients:

- 8 oz elbow macaroni
- 2 cups shredded sharp cheddar cheese
- 1/2 cup grated Parmesan cheese
- 2 cups whole milk
- 2 tbsp butter
- 2 tbsp all-purpose flour
- 4 slices bacon (crispy and crumbled)
- 1 cup fresh spinach (sautéed)
- Salt and pepper to taste

Instructions:

1. Cook the macaroni according to package instructions, drain, and set aside.
2. In a skillet, sauté the spinach in a little butter until wilted. Set aside.
3. In the same skillet, cook the bacon until crispy. Crumble the bacon and set aside.
4. In a saucepan, melt the butter over medium heat. Stir in the flour and cook for 1-2 minutes.
5. Gradually whisk in the milk, and cook for 3-5 minutes until the sauce thickens.
6. Stir in the cheddar, Parmesan, salt, and pepper. Once the cheese has melted, fold in the bacon and spinach.

7. Toss the cooked macaroni in the cheese sauce and bacon-spinach mixture, and serve warm.

Mac and Cheese with Roasted Cauliflower

Ingredients:

- 8 oz elbow macaroni
- 2 cups shredded sharp cheddar cheese
- 1/2 cup grated Parmesan cheese
- 2 cups whole milk
- 2 tbsp butter
- 2 tbsp all-purpose flour
- 1 head of cauliflower (cut into florets)
- 2 tbsp olive oil
- Salt and pepper to taste

Instructions:

1. Preheat the oven to 400°F (200°C). Toss the cauliflower florets with olive oil, salt, and pepper. Roast for 20-25 minutes until golden and tender.
2. Cook the macaroni according to package instructions, drain, and set aside.
3. In a saucepan, melt the butter over medium heat. Stir in the flour and cook for 1-2 minutes.
4. Gradually whisk in the milk, and cook for 3-5 minutes until the sauce thickens.
5. Stir in the cheddar, Parmesan, salt, and pepper. Once the cheese has melted, fold in the roasted cauliflower.

6. Toss the cooked macaroni in the cheese sauce and cauliflower mixture, and serve warm.

Mac and Cheese with Gouda and Bacon

Ingredients:

- 8 oz elbow macaroni
- 2 cups shredded Gouda cheese
- 1/2 cup grated Parmesan cheese
- 2 cups whole milk
- 2 tbsp butter
- 2 tbsp all-purpose flour
- 4 slices bacon (crispy and crumbled)
- Salt and pepper to taste

Instructions:

1. Cook the macaroni according to package instructions, drain, and set aside.
2. In a skillet, cook the bacon until crispy. Crumble the bacon and set aside.
3. In a saucepan, melt the butter over medium heat. Stir in the flour and cook for 1-2 minutes.
4. Gradually whisk in the milk, and cook for 3-5 minutes until the sauce thickens.
5. Stir in the Gouda, Parmesan, salt, and pepper. Once the cheese has melted, fold in the crumbled bacon.
6. Toss the cooked macaroni in the cheese sauce and bacon mixture, and serve warm.

Vegan Mac and Cheese

Ingredients:

- 8 oz elbow macaroni
- 1 cup raw cashews (soaked for at least 4 hours)
- 1/2 cup nutritional yeast
- 1/2 cup unsweetened almond milk
- 2 tbsp olive oil
- 2 tbsp lemon juice
- 1 tsp garlic powder
- 1 tsp onion powder
- Salt and pepper to taste

Instructions:

1. Cook the macaroni according to package instructions, drain, and set aside.
2. In a blender, combine the soaked cashews, nutritional yeast, almond milk, olive oil, lemon juice, garlic powder, onion powder, salt, and pepper. Blend until smooth and creamy.
3. Toss the cooked macaroni with the vegan cheese sauce and serve warm.

Mac and Cheese with Lobster and Crab

Ingredients:

- 8 oz elbow macaroni
- 2 cups shredded sharp cheddar cheese
- 1/2 cup grated Parmesan cheese
- 2 cups whole milk
- 2 tbsp butter
- 2 tbsp all-purpose flour
- 1 cup cooked lobster meat (chopped)
- 1/2 cup cooked crab meat (chopped)
- Salt and pepper to taste

Instructions:

1. Cook the macaroni according to package instructions, drain, and set aside.
2. In a saucepan, melt the butter over medium heat. Stir in the flour and cook for 1-2 minutes.
3. Gradually whisk in the milk, and cook for 3-5 minutes until the sauce thickens.
4. Stir in the cheddar, Parmesan, salt, and pepper. Once the cheese has melted, fold in the lobster and crab meat.
5. Toss the cooked macaroni in the seafood cheese sauce, and serve warm.

Mac and Cheese with Duck Confit

Ingredients:

- 8 oz elbow macaroni
- 2 cups shredded Gruyère cheese
- 1/2 cup grated Parmesan cheese
- 2 cups whole milk
- 2 tbsp butter
- 2 tbsp all-purpose flour
- 2 duck legs (confit)
- Salt and pepper to taste

Instructions:

1. Cook the macaroni according to package instructions, drain, and set aside.
2. In a skillet, heat the duck confit over medium heat until crispy. Shred the meat and set aside.
3. In a saucepan, melt the butter over medium heat. Stir in the flour and cook for 1-2 minutes.
4. Gradually whisk in the milk, and cook for 3-5 minutes until the sauce thickens.
5. Stir in the Gruyère, Parmesan, salt, and pepper. Once the cheese has melted, fold in the shredded duck confit.
6. Toss the cooked macaroni in the cheese sauce and duck confit mixture, and serve warm.

Mac and Cheese with Applewood Smoked Bacon

Ingredients:

- 8 oz elbow macaroni
- 2 cups shredded sharp cheddar cheese
- 1/2 cup grated Parmesan cheese
- 2 cups whole milk
- 2 tbsp butter
- 2 tbsp all-purpose flour
- 6 slices applewood smoked bacon (crispy and crumbled)
- Salt and pepper to taste

Instructions:

1. Cook the macaroni according to package instructions, drain, and set aside.
2. In a skillet, cook the bacon until crispy. Crumble the bacon and set aside.
3. In a saucepan, melt the butter over medium heat. Stir in the flour and cook for 1-2 minutes.
4. Gradually whisk in the milk, and cook for 3-5 minutes until the sauce thickens.
5. Stir in the cheddar, Parmesan, salt, and pepper. Once the cheese has melted, fold in the crumbled bacon.
6. Toss the cooked macaroni in the cheese sauce and bacon mixture, and serve warm.

Mac and Cheese with Kale and Sausage

Ingredients:

- 8 oz elbow macaroni
- 2 cups shredded sharp cheddar cheese
- 1/2 cup grated Parmesan cheese
- 2 cups whole milk
- 2 tbsp butter
- 2 tbsp all-purpose flour
- 2 sausages (your choice, cooked and crumbled)
- 1 cup kale (washed and chopped)
- Salt and pepper to taste

Instructions:

1. Cook the macaroni according to package instructions, drain, and set aside.
2. In a skillet, cook the sausage until browned. Set aside.
3. In the same skillet, sauté the kale until wilted. Set aside.
4. In a saucepan, melt the butter over medium heat. Stir in the flour and cook for 1-2 minutes.
5. Gradually whisk in the milk, and cook for 3-5 minutes until the sauce thickens.
6. Stir in the cheddar, Parmesan, salt, and pepper. Once the cheese has melted, fold in the sausage and kale.

7. Toss the cooked macaroni in the cheese sauce and sausage-kale mixture, and serve warm.

Mac and Cheese with Sweet Corn and Jalapeños

Ingredients:

- 8 oz elbow macaroni
- 2 cups shredded sharp cheddar cheese
- 1/2 cup grated Parmesan cheese
- 2 cups whole milk
- 2 tbsp butter
- 2 tbsp all-purpose flour
- 1 cup sweet corn (frozen or fresh)
- 1-2 jalapeños (sliced)
- Salt and pepper to taste

Instructions:

1. Cook the macaroni according to package instructions, drain, and set aside.
2. In a saucepan, melt the butter over medium heat. Stir in the flour and cook for 1-2 minutes.
3. Gradually whisk in the milk, and cook for 3-5 minutes until the sauce thickens.
4. Stir in the cheddar, Parmesan, salt, and pepper. Once the cheese has melted, fold in the corn and sliced jalapeños.
5. Toss the cooked macaroni in the cheese sauce and corn-jalapeño mixture, and serve warm.

www.ingramcontent.com/pod-product-compliance
Lightning Source LLC
LaVergne TN
LVHW081318060526
838201LV00055B/2336